HOME OWNERSHIP IS CLOSER THAN YOU THINK:

When You Have Will, You Have A Way

Written By

Willie Adolph

DEDICATION

I dedicate this book, first and foremost, to my incredible wife, Tikila. Your unconditional support through every high, every low, and all the "crazy" moments in between has been my anchor. You are my strength, my partner, and my greatest blessing.

To our children and grandchildren — thank you for patiently listening to my life "suggestions." You are my legacy, and it is for you that I strive to be better every day.

To our parents — thank you for being our solid foundation, always there when the path grew narrow and times were tough. Your love and support have meant more than words can express.

And finally, to you — the reader — thank you for giving another "real estate book" a chance. I hope these pages not only inform you but also inspire you to take bold steps toward your dreams.

HOME OWNERSHIP IS CLOSER THAN YOU THINK
When You Have Will, You Have A Way

Written By
Willie Adolph

Fullcover Design By
Sun Child Wind Spirit

Proofread By
Tikila Antoinette Adolph

Edited By
Mylia Tiye Mal Jaza

Author Contact
TheAdolphs.com
Tikila & Willie Adolph
(281) 451-7087
customerservice@TheAdolphs.com
bit.ly/theadolphs

Self-Publishing Associate
BePublished.Org - Chicago 60602
Dr. Mary M. Jefferson
(972) 880-8316
www.bepublished.biz
mari@bepublished.org

First Edition.
Printed In the USA. Recycled Paper Encouraged.

TABLE OF CONTENT

(MORE)

TOC (cont'd)

FOREWORD
By Tikila Antoinette Adolph

It is with immense pride, love, and joy that I write this foreword for my husband, Willie.

Anyone who knows Willie knows that staying still to focus on just one thing — especially something as demanding as writing a book — is not his natural rhythm. His creative mind is always buzzing, dreaming big, moving toward the next big idea. And yet, here he is, holding this incredible achievement in his hands. I'm so proud of him for seeing this through to the finish line.

Willie and I have shared over 25 beautiful years of marriage, raising four amazing children, two wonderful grandchildren, and, of course, our sweet dog, Dash. For over three decades, we've built businesses side by side — from selling cell phones and pagers, running daycares, telemarketing all kinds of products, to becoming trusted loan officers, and now, respected Real Estate Experts and Advisors. We've lived every chapter together: growing, learning, stumbling at times, but always moving forward, hand in hand.

Willie is my soulmate, my life partner, my business partner, my best friend, and the leader of our home. It is an honor to walk by his side, supporting him as his suitable helper, just as it was beautifully designed:

"Then the LORD God said, 'It is not good for the man to be alone; I will make a helper suitable for him.'" — Genesis 2:18.

We are far from perfect, but we complement each other in a way only God could have orchestrated.

Willie's mind is a masterpiece of creativity. He is a marketing genius, a master negotiator, and a real-life Superman, helping and rescuing people both personally and professionally. Every day, my admiration for him deepens. Watching him pour his heart, knowledge, and experience into this book has only increased my respect and excitement for everything still to come. I am so grateful that you have decided to read this book, and I pray that you take notes, purchase your dream home, and share this book with someone else.

I'm incredibly proud of him and I look forward to the many more books he will write, the countless people he will continue to inspire, and the adventures that still lie ahead. I love doing life with my person, and I wouldn't trade it for anything.

Congratulations, Willie. The world is better because you're in it — and now, your words will help even more people find their way into homeownership.

As you embark on this new chapter with the completion of this book, I'm excited to see where your boundless creativity and determination will take you. I know this is just the beginning of a journey that will continue to inspire others and leave a lasting impact.

I love living life with you, Willie, and I wouldn't have it any other way.

Here's to the future and all the amazing things still to come.

With love, admiration, and gratitude,
Tikila, your Wifey

Introduction to Homebuying
Your Guide to Making
a Smart Investment

Buying a home is one of the most significant financial and emotional decisions you'll make in your lifetime. Whether you're a first-time homebuyer or someone looking to purchase a new property, the journey to homeownership requires careful planning, informed decision-making, and a solid understanding of the process.

This guide will walk you through the key aspects of home buying, helping you assess your readiness, understand the financial implications, and navigate each step with confidence.

Understanding the Decision to Buy a Home

The decision to buy a home is not just about finding the perfect property—it's about making a long-term commitment that aligns with your financial goals, lifestyle, and future plans. Before jumping into the process, it's important to evaluate why you want to buy a home and whether it's the right time for you.

1. The Benefits of Homeownership

Owning a home offers several advantages compared to renting. Some of the key benefits include:

- Building Equity: Each mortgage payment you make contributes to building equity, which is the portion of the home you truly own. Over time, this can become a significant financial asset.

- Long-Term Investment: Real estate generally appreciates over time, meaning your home could increase in value, allowing you to profit when you sell.

- Stability and Control: Homeownership gives you control over your living space—no more rent increases, lease renewals, or landlord restrictions.

- Tax Benefits: Many homeowners qualify for tax deductions, including mortgage interest and property taxes, which can reduce your taxable income.

• Personalization: Unlike renting, owning a home allows you to renovate, remodel, and personalize your space to suit your style and needs.

2. Is Buying a Home Right for You?

While homeownership comes with many perks, it's not the right choice for everyone. Before committing to buying a home, consider the following:

• How long do you plan to stay in the home? If you're planning to move within a few years, renting may be a better option. Buying a home makes the most financial sense when you stay in it long enough to build equity and cover transaction costs.

• Are you ready for the responsibilities of homeownership? Owning a home means handling maintenance, repairs, and other responsibilities that landlords typically cover for renters.

• Can you afford the upfront and ongoing costs? Beyond the purchase price, homeownership involves additional expenses such as property taxes, insurance, utilities, and maintenance.

Chapter 1
Assessing Personal & Financial Readiness

Buying a home is a significant financial commitment, so it's essential to evaluate your readiness before taking the plunge. Here's how to assess whether you're financially and personally prepared for homeownership.

1. Evaluating Your Financial Health

Your financial situation plays a crucial role in determining whether you can afford to buy a home. Consider the following:

A. Credit Score and History

Your credit score is one of the most important factors lenders consider when approving a mortgage. A higher credit score can help you secure better loan terms, including lower interest rates.

• Check your credit score: Lenders typically look for a credit score of at least 620 for conventional loans, though higher scores (700+) may qualify you for better rates.

• Review your credit report: Ensure there are no errors or outstanding debts that could negatively impact your mortgage application.

• Improve your credit score if needed: Pay down debts, make timely payments, and avoid opening new credit accounts before applying for a mortgage.

B. Savings and Down Payment

Having sufficient savings is crucial when buying a home. You'll need funds for:

• Down payment: Most conventional loans require a down payment of 5% to 20% of the home's purchase price. FHA loans allow for as little as 3.5% down for qualified buyers.

• Closing costs: These typically range from 2% to 5% of the home's purchase price and cover fees for the lender, appraisal, title insurance, and other expenses.

• Emergency fund: It's wise to have additional savings to cover unexpected home repairs or financial challenges.

C. Debt-to-Income Ratio (DTI)

Lenders assess your ability to repay a mortgage by looking at your debt-to-income (DTI) ratio. A lower DTI ratio increases your chances of loan approval.

• DTI calculation: (Total monthly debt payments ÷ Gross monthly income) × 100

• Ideal DTI for mortgage approval: Most lenders prefer a DTI of 43% or lower, though some may accept higher ratios depending on other financial factors.

D. Pre-Approval for a Mortgage

Getting pre-approved for a mortgage helps determine how much you can afford and shows sellers that you're a serious buyer. The pre-approval process involves:

- Submitting financial documents (pay stubs, tax returns, bank statements)

- A credit check by the lender

- Determining the maximum loan amount you qualify for

2. Considering Your Lifestyle and Future Plans

Beyond finances, think about how homeownership fits into your long-term plans.

- Job stability: Is your employment stable, or do you anticipate relocating soon?

- Family considerations: Are you planning to start or expand your family, which might require a larger home?

• Preferred location: Do you want to live in a city, suburb, or rural area? Consider commute times, school districts, and amenities.

Overview of the Home-Buying Process

Understanding the steps involved in purchasing a home can help you navigate the process with confidence. Here's a general overview:

1. Define Your Home Buying Criteria

Consider what features are most important to you, such as:

- Home type: Single-family home, condo, townhouse, etc.

- Size and layout: Number of bedrooms, bathrooms, square footage.

- Location: Proximity to work, schools, public transportation, and amenities.

- Neighborhood features: Safety, community vibe, future development plans.

2. Get Pre-Approved for a Mortgage

As mentioned earlier, pre-approval helps determine your budget and strengthens your position as a buyer.

3. Work with a Real Estate Agent

An experienced real estate agent can:

- ✓ Help you find homes that match your criteria.
- ✓ Provide market insights and neighborhood information.
- ✓ Negotiate on your behalf to get the best deal.
- ✓ Guide you through paperwork and closing.

4. Start House Hunting

Once you're pre-approved, you can start visiting properties. During showings, consider:

- The home's condition (check for necessary repairs).

- The neighborhood's atmosphere.

- Future resale value potential.

5. Make an Offer

When you find the right home, you'll submit an offer that includes:

- The purchase price.

- Any contingencies (home inspection, financing, appraisal).

- Closing date preferences.

The seller may accept, reject, or counter your offer.

6. Home Inspection and Appraisal

After your offer is accepted:

- Home inspection: Identifies potential issues or repairs needed before finalizing the purchase.

• Appraisal: Confirms the home's value aligns with your loan amount.

7. Secure Financing and Finalize Mortgage

Your lender will finalize your mortgage, ensuring all documents are in order for closing.

8. Closing Process

Closing is the final step where you sign all necessary documents and officially take ownership. Be prepared to:

• Pay closing costs.

• Review and sign legal documents.

• Receive the keys to your new home!

Final Thoughts

Buying a home is an exciting milestone that requires careful preparation and informed decision-making. By understanding the key factors in homeownership, assessing your financial readiness, and familiarizing yourself with the home-buying process, you can make a smart and confident investment in your future.

Chapter 2
Preparing for Home Ownership

Now that you understand the key considerations behind the decision to buy a home, it's time to dive deeper into the financial aspects of homeownership. Proper financial preparation ensures that you're not only able to purchase a home but also sustain homeownership comfortably without financial strain.

This chapter will guide you through evaluating your financial health, understanding the importance of credit scores, determining your budget, and ensuring you are financially prepared to make a confident and well-informed home purchase.

Evaluating Your Financial Situation

Before embarking on your home-buying journey, a thorough evaluation of your financial health is crucial. This includes assessing your income, savings, debt, and long-term financial stability.

1. Understanding Your Income and Stability

A stable and sufficient income is key to qualifying for a mortgage and managing homeownership costs. Consider:

- Job stability: Lenders prefer borrowers with consistent employment history, ideally at least two years in the same job or industry.

- Future earning potential: Will your income likely increase, remain stable, or fluctuate?

- Additional sources of income: Bonuses, side jobs, or rental income can enhance your financial profile.

2. Assessing Your Savings

Homeownership comes with upfront and ongoing costs, making it essential to have savings in place. Evaluate:

- Down payment savings: Most conventional loans require 5%-20% down, while FHA loans may allow as low as 3.5%.

- Closing costs: Typically range from 2%-5% of the home's purchase price and cover lender fees, title insurance, and more.

- Emergency fund: Experts recommend having 3-6 months of living expenses saved for unexpected repairs, job loss, or other emergencies.

3. Reviewing Your Debt and Monthly Expenses

Lenders assess your debt-to-income ratio (DTI) to determine if you can afford a mortgage. To calculate your DTI:

(Total monthly debt payments ÷ Gross monthly income) × 100 = DTI%

• Ideal DTI ratio: Most lenders prefer a DTI of 43% or lower. A lower ratio improves your chances of mortgage approval.

• Reducing debt: Paying down credit cards, car loans, or student loans before applying for a mortgage can help improve your DTI.

Importance of Credit Scores and How to Improve Them

Your credit score plays a significant role in determining your mortgage eligibility, interest rate, and loan terms.

1. What Credit Score Do You Need to Buy a Home?

Different mortgage loan types have varying credit score requirements:

• Conventional Loan: Minimum credit score of 620 (higher scores qualify for better rates).

• FHA Loan: Minimum score of 580 (or 500 with a 10% down payment).

• VA Loan: No set minimum, but most lenders look for 620+.

• USDA Loan: Typically requires a 640+ score.

A higher credit score can save you thousands over the life of your mortgage by securing a lower interest rate.

2. How to Check Your Credit Score

• Obtain a free credit report from AnnualCreditReport.com (available once per year from Equifax, Experian, and TransUnion).

• Review your report for errors and dispute any incorrect information.

3. Steps to Improve Your Credit Score

If your credit score needs improvement, take these steps before applying for a mortgage:

• Make payments on time: Payment history accounts for 35% of your credit score.

• Lower your credit utilization: Aim to use less than 30% of your available credit.

• Pay down existing debt: Reduce credit card balances and avoid new debt.

• Avoid opening new credit accounts: Multiple new credit inquiries can lower your score.

• Keep old accounts open: Length of credit history matters—closing old accounts can negatively impact your score.

Improving your credit score takes time, so start as early as possible before beginning the home-buying process.

Determining Your Budget and Affordability

Before searching for homes, it's crucial to establish how much you can afford to spend. Your budget should align with both your mortgage qualification and your lifestyle.

1. The 28/36 Rule: A General Guideline

Lenders use the 28/36 rule to determine affordability:

- No more than 28% of your gross monthly income should go toward housing expenses (mortgage, taxes, insurance).

- No more than 36% of your gross income should go toward total debt payments (including credit cards, student loans, car loans).

For example, if your gross monthly income is $6,000, your home-related expenses should not exceed $1,680 (28%), and total debts should stay under $2,160 (36%).

2. Hidden Costs of Homeownership

Beyond the mortgage, consider additional costs:

- Property taxes: Varies by location and home value.

• Homeowners insurance: Required by lenders and depends on location and home features.

• HOA fees: If buying in a community with a homeowners association.

• Utilities: Electricity, water, gas, internet, and trash services.

• Maintenance and repairs: Set aside 1-3% of the home's value annually for upkeep.

3. Mortgage Pre-Approval: How Much Can You Borrow?

Getting pre-approved for a mortgage gives you an idea of how much a lender is willing to offer based on your financial profile. To get pre-approved, you'll need:

• Proof of income (pay stubs, tax returns, W-2s).

• Bank statements and asset documentation.

• Credit report and score.

• Employment verification.

Checklist: Financial Preparedness
for Buying a Home

Before starting your home search, use this checklist to ensure you're financially prepared:

✅ Credit Score & History

• Check your credit report for accuracy.

• Aim for a credit score of 620+ (higher is better).

• Pay off outstanding debts and lower credit utilization.

✅ Savings & Emergency Fund

• Save enough for a down payment (5%-20% for conventional loans, 3.5% for FHA loans).

• Have funds for closing costs (2%-5% of the home's purchase price).

• Maintain an emergency fund for at least 3-6 months of expenses.

✅ Debt-to-Income Ratio (DTI)

• Ensure your DTI is below 43% for mortgage approval.

• Pay down high-interest debts to improve affordability.

✅ Stable Income & Employment

• Maintain steady employment for at least 2 years in the same field.

• Have consistent income sources with documented proof.

✅ Budget & Affordability

• Follow the 28/36 rule to determine a comfortable mortgage payment.

• Account for additional homeownership costs like property taxes, insurance, and maintenance.

✅ Mortgage Pre-Approval

• Get pre-approved by a lender to determine your borrowing power.

• Gather necessary documents (income proof, bank statements, tax returns).

Final Thoughts

Preparing for homeownership is more than just saving for a down payment—it requires careful evaluation of your financial situation, improving your credit, and ensuring you can comfortably afford your future home. By taking the necessary steps outlined in this chapter, you'll set yourself up for success and enter the home-buying process with confidence.

In the next chapter, we'll explore house hunting strategies, choosing the right home, and making a competitive offer.

Remember, When You Have Will, You Have a Way. My Name Is Will. Let's get you financially ready for your dream home!

Whether you're just starting to explore the idea of buying a home or actively searching for properties, working with knowledgeable professionals—such as a trusted real estate agent and mortgage lender—can make all the difference.

When you're ready to take the next step, remember: When You Have Will, You Have a Way. My Name Is Will. Let's find your dream home together!

Chapter 3
Understanding the Houston Housing Market

Buying a home is a significant investment, and understanding the local real estate market is essential for making an informed decision. The Houston housing market is diverse, dynamic, and influenced by various economic and demographic factors. Whether you're a first-time homebuyer or looking to upgrade, having a solid grasp of current market trends, key influences, and neighborhood characteristics will help you make a smart investment.

In this chapter, we'll explore Houston's market trends, factors affecting home prices, neighborhood selection, and how to research the local market effectively.

Current Market Trends in Houston and Surrounding Areas

The Houston housing market is known for its resilience and steady growth. Understanding its current trends can help buyers make better purchasing decisions.

1. Market Overview

Houston is one of the largest and fastest-growing metropolitan areas in the U.S., offering a mix of urban, suburban, and rural housing options. The market trends can vary depending on economic conditions, interest rates, and housing inventory. Here are key factors shaping Houston's real estate market:

- Home Prices: Prices have seen consistent appreciation, but affordability remains better than in other major U.S. cities.

- Inventory Levels: A balance between supply and demand dictates whether it's a buyer's or seller's market.

• Mortgage Rates: Interest rates significantly impact affordability and demand.

• New Construction: Houston continues to expand with new developments, providing more options for homebuyers.

• Rental Market: A strong rental market influences home values, as investors seek properties with high rental potential.

2. Is It a Buyer's or Seller's Market?

The balance of supply and demand determines whether buyers or sellers have the advantage:

• Buyer's Market: More homes for sale than buyers, leading to better deals and negotiation power.

• Seller's Market: High demand with limited inventory, resulting in competitive bidding and higher prices.

Understanding where Houston stands in this cycle can help you strategize your home purchase.

3. Seasonal Trends

Like most markets, real estate activity in Houston fluctuates throughout the year:

• Spring & Summer: Peak buying and selling season, leading to higher prices and competition.

• Fall & Winter: Slower months with potential for better deals.

Factors Influencing the Local Real Estate Market

Several factors contribute to Houston's real estate trends, influencing home prices and availability.

1. Economy & Job Growth

Houston's economy is fueled by industries such as:

• Energy & Oil: A major driver of employment and real estate demand.

• Healthcare & Biotechnology: A growing sector attracting professionals.

• Aerospace & Technology: Further diversifying Houston's economy.

A strong job market attracts more residents, increasing demand for housing.

2. Population Growth & Migration Trends

Houston continues to see population growth due to:

• Affordable cost of living compared to other major cities.

• No state income tax, attracting out-of-state buyers.

• Job opportunities, leading to relocation from other states.

This growth creates a consistent demand for housing.

3. Interest Rates & Lending Environment

Mortgage interest rates play a crucial role in affordability. When rates are low, demand increases, pushing home prices higher. When rates rise, affordability decreases, slowing market activity. Staying informed on interest rate trends can help you time your purchase.

4. Natural Disasters & Climate Considerations

Houston's real estate market is influenced by:

• Flood Zones: Some areas are prone to flooding; flood insurance may be required.

• Hurricane Season: Weather risks impact home values and insurance costs.

Understanding these risks helps buyers make informed location decisions.

Neighborhood Analysis and Selection

Choosing the right neighborhood is just as important as selecting the right home. Consider factors such as home values, school districts, commute times, and community amenities.

1. Types of Neighborhoods in Houston

Houston offers a variety of communities to suit different lifestyles:

• Urban Living: The Heights, Midtown, Downtown – Ideal for professionals seeking walkability and entertainment.

• Suburban Comfort: Katy, Sugar Land, Cypress – Great for families looking for top-rated schools and spacious homes.

• Luxury & Gated Communities: River Oaks, The Woodlands, Memorial – High-end properties with exclusive amenities.

• Affordable & Up-and-Coming Areas: Spring Branch, East Downtown (EaDo), Independence Heights – More affordable options with growth potential.

2. Factors to Consider When Choosing a Neighborhood

When evaluating neighborhoods, consider:

• Affordability: Does it fit your budget and long-term financial goals?

• School Districts: Important for families and resale value.

• Commute & Transportation: Proximity to work, highways, and public transit.

• Safety & Crime Rates: Research crime statistics for peace of mind.

• Amenities & Lifestyle: Parks, restaurants, shopping, and entertainment.

• Future Growth & Development: Areas with planned infrastructure improvements may increase in value.

3. Researching Property Values & Market Trends

Use online tools and resources such as:

• HAR.com (Houston Association of Realtors) – Local MLS listings and market insights.

• Zillow & Redfin – Home price trends and neighborhood data.

• City of Houston Planning & Development – Future development plans and zoning changes.

Speaking with local real estate professionals can also provide valuable insights into Houston's evolving market.

Checklist: Researching the Houston Market

Use this checklist to ensure you have a thorough understanding of Houston's housing market before making a purchase:

✅ Understand Market Trends

• Research whether it's a buyer's or seller's market.

• Stay updated on home price trends and inventory levels.

• Track mortgage rate changes to determine affordability.

✅ Analyze Market Influences

• Consider job growth and economic factors affecting demand.

• Evaluate how population growth impacts housing supply.

• Factor in climate risks (flood zones, hurricanes).

✅ Choose the Right Neighborhood

• Compare different areas based on affordability and lifestyle.

- Check school district ratings and future development plans.

- Research crime rates and community amenities.

✅ **Assess Home Value & Investment Potential**

- Review recent home sales and appreciation rates.

- Investigate planned infrastructure and commercial growth.

- Work with a local real estate expert for insider knowledge.

Final Thoughts

Understanding Houston's housing market is key to making a sound investment. By researching current trends, evaluating influential factors, and selecting the right neighborhood, you can confidently navigate the home-buying process.

In the next chapter, we'll dive into the home search process, what to look for during showings, and how to make a strong offer.

Remember, "When You Have Will, You Have a Way." My Name Is Will. Let's find your perfect home in Houston!

Chapter 4
The Role of Real Estate Agents

Buying a home is one of the most significant financial and emotional decisions you'll make. While some buyers consider navigating the process alone, working with a professional real estate agent can make the journey smoother, faster, and more successful. In this chapter, we'll explore:

✓ The 101 benefits of hiring a real estate agent

✓ How agents assist throughout the home-buying process

✓ The unique advantages of having an agent when purchasing a new construction home

✓ A step-by-step checklist for choosing the right agent

101 Benefits of Hiring a Real Estate Agent

A skilled real estate agent brings expertise, experience, and negotiation skills to the table, helping buyers make informed decisions. Below are 101 key benefits of working with a real estate agent.

1.   Expertise & Market Knowledge

1. Access to real-time market data

2. Knowledge of local neighborhoods

3. Insights on property values and future appreciation

4. Understanding of buyer and seller market trends

5. Advice on best times to buy

2. Time & Convenience

6. Handles property searches based on your needs

7. Schedules and organizes home showings

8. Saves you hours of online research

9. Coordinates with lenders, inspectors, and title companies

10. Works around your schedule

3. Negotiation Skills

11. Negotiates the best purchase price

12. Helps with seller concessions (closing costs, repairs, etc.)

13. Protects you from overpaying

14. Prepares competitive offers

15. Handles bidding wars with strategic counteroffers

4. Financial Guidance & Connections

16. Provides insight into mortgage options

17. Helps you understand loan pre-approvals vs. pre-qualifications

18. Refers trusted mortgage lenders

19. Identifies down payment assistance programs

20. Helps estimate closing costs

5. Due Diligence & Paperwork

21. Reviews contracts and disclosures

22. Helps with offer letters and contingencies

23. Ensures legal compliance

24. Guides you through inspections and appraisals

25. Manages all transaction deadlines

6. Avoiding Pitfalls & Mistakes

26. Identifies red flags in properties

27. Helps you avoid costly repair surprises

28. Advises on flood zones and insurance requirements

29. Ensures you don't overlook crucial details

30. Protects you from scams or bad deals

For sake of time, I will circle back to this at another date. The remaining 71 benefits will help you have a total of 101 reasons to select a skilled real estate agent to assist you with your process. I really could write a whole book on this topic itself. I might just do that if I don't have a chance to add the remaining 71 here before publishing.

How Agents Assist in the Home-Buying Process

A real estate agent plays a crucial role at every stage of your home-buying journey.

1. Home Search & Selection

- Helps you define your needs vs. wants
- Sends personalized home listings
- Arranges and attends property showings
- Provides insights on comparable homes in the area

2. Offer & Negotiation

- Advises on the best offer price
- Includes key contract contingencies to protect you
- Negotiates with sellers and their agents
- Reviews inspection and appraisal results

3. Closing Process

- Works with lenders and title companies

- Helps you understand closing costs and documents

- Ensures final walkthroughs go smoothly

- Makes sure you close on time

Your agent acts as your advisor, advocate, and negotiator, ensuring you get the best deal while avoiding stress and costly mistakes.

Specific Advantages When Purchasing New Construction Homes

Buying a new construction home is different from purchasing a resale property. Builders have their own contracts, pricing strategies, and incentives—having a real estate agent on your side can save you money and protect your interests.

1. Representation & Negotiation

- Builder sales reps work for the builder, not you. An agent ensures your best interests are prioritized.

- Agents negotiate for upgrades, incentives, and better pricing.

2. Understanding Builder Contracts

- New home contracts differ from traditional real estate contracts.

- Your agent explains terms, timelines, and cancellation policies.

3. Inspections & Quality Control

- Agents recommend third-party inspections (even for new homes).

- They help identify construction defects before closing.

4. Financing & Incentives
- Builders offer their own financing options, but an agent helps you compare lenders for the best deal.

• They make sure you maximize incentives without hidden trade-offs.

Having an agent ensures you don't overpay and receive top value for your investment.

Checklist: Selecting the Right Real Estate Agent

Use this checklist to find the best agent for your home-buying journey.

☑ Experience & Knowledge

☐ Specializes in buyer representation

☐ Familiar with Houston's market and neighborhoods

☐ Knows new construction home buying

☑ Communication & Availability

☐ Responsive to calls, texts, and emails

☐ Takes time to explain the process

☐ Works around your schedule

☑ Reputation & Reviews

☐ Positive client testimonials and referrals

☐ Strong track record of successful transactions

☐ Knowledgeable about negotiation strategies

☑ Professional Network

☐ Has connections with lenders, inspectors, and title companies

☐ Can recommend contractors, movers, and other services

☑ Personality & Trust

☐ Listens to your needs and goals

☐ Makes you feel comfortable and confident

☐ Is genuinely committed to helping you find the perfect home

Final Thoughts

Choosing the right real estate agent is one of the most important decisions in your home-buying journey. A skilled agent makes the process easier, protects your interests, and ensures you get the best deal.

In the next chapter, we'll dive into finding the perfect home, understanding property types, and making a strong offer.

When You Have Will, You Have a Way. My Name Is Will. Let's find your dream home together!

Chapter 5
Financing Your Home Purchase

Financing is one of the most crucial aspects of purchasing a home. Understanding your mortgage options, navigating the pre-approval process, and knowing how interest rates impact your loan can empower you to make confident financial decisions.

In this chapter, we'll cover:

☑ Exploring mortgage options

☑ The pre-approval process

☑ Understanding interest rates and loan terms

☑ Checklist: Mortgage application process

Exploring Mortgage Options

When buying a home, most people rely on a mortgage—a loan specifically for purchasing property. There are several types of mortgages, each with different advantages depending on your financial situation.

1. Conventional Loans

- Best for: Buyers with good credit and a solid down payment.

- Down Payment: Typically 3% to 20%.

- Pros: Lower overall borrowing costs, no upfront mortgage insurance (with 20% down).

- Cons: Stricter credit requirements.

2. FHA Loans (Federal Housing Administration)

- Best for: First-time homebuyers or those with lower credit scores.

- Down Payment: As low as 3.5%.

• Pros: Easier qualification, lower down payment.

• Cons: Requires mortgage insurance (MIP) for the life of the loan.

3. VA Loans (Veterans Affairs)

• Best for: Active-duty military, veterans, and eligible spouses.

• Down Payment: None required.

• Pros: No down payment, no private mortgage insurance (PMI).

• Cons: Must meet military service requirements.

4. USDA Loans (United States Department of Agriculture)

• Best for: Buyers in rural or suburban areas.

• Down Payment: None required.

• Pros: Low interest rates, no down payment.

• Cons: Property must be in a USDA-eligible area.

5. Jumbo Loans

• Best for: Buyers purchasing high-priced luxury homes.

• Loan Amount: Above conventional loan limits (currently $766,550 for most areas in 2024).

• Pros: Access to financing for expensive properties.

• Cons: Higher interest rates and stricter qualifications.

The Pre-Approval Process

Getting pre-approved for a mortgage is a critical step in the home-buying process. It shows sellers you are a serious buyer and helps you understand how much home you can afford.

1. Pre-Qualification vs. Pre-Approval

• Pre-Qualification: An estimate of how much you may be able to borrow based on basic financial information. Quick and informal.

• Pre-Approval: A formal evaluation by a lender that verifies your financial details and provides a conditional loan amount. Stronger than pre-qualification.

2. Steps in the Pre-Approval Process:

1. Gather Financial Documents:

- Recent pay stubs

- Tax returns (last 2 years)

- Bank statements

- W-2 or 1099 forms

- Credit report

2. Submit Your Application: Complete a mortgage application with a lender.

3. Credit Check: Lenders will pull your credit report to assess your score and history.

4. Lender Review: The lender reviews your debt-to-income ratio (DTI), assets, and employment history.

5. Receive Your Pre-Approval Letter: The letter states how much you are approved to borrow, which you can use to make strong offers on homes.

Understanding Interest Rates and Loan Terms

1. How Interest Rates Affect Your Mortgage

The interest rate is the cost of borrowing money from your lender. Even a small difference in rates can significantly impact your monthly payment and the total cost of your loan.

Fixed-Rate Mortgage:

• Interest rate stays the same for the life of the loan.

• Best for: Buyers planning to stay in their home long-term.

• Typical Terms: 15, 20, or 30 years.

Adjustable-Rate Mortgage (ARM):

• Interest rate is fixed for an initial period, then adjusts annually.

• Best for: Buyers who plan to sell or refinance before the rate adjusts.

• Example: 5/1 ARM means a fixed rate for 5 years, then adjusts yearly.

2. Loan Terms and Their Impact on Monthly Payments

• 15-Year Loan: Higher monthly payments but less interest paid over time.

• 30-Year Loan: Lower monthly payments but more interest paid over time.

3. Factors Affecting Your Mortgage Interest Rate:

• Credit Score: Higher scores qualify for better rates.

• Loan Amount and Down Payment: Larger down payments can lower your rate.

• Loan Type: VA and USDA loans often have lower rates.

• Market Conditions: Rates fluctuate based on the economy.

Checklist: Mortgage Application Process

Use this checklist to navigate the mortgage application process smoothly:

☑ 1. Find a Lender:

☐ Research lenders or get referrals from your real estate agent.

☐ Compare rates and loan options.

☐ Ask about closing costs and fees.

☑ 2. Get Pre-Approved:

☐ Submit financial documents (pay stubs, tax returns, bank statements).

☐ Authorize a credit check.

☐ Obtain your pre-approval letter.

☑ 3. Select a Loan Program:

☐ Compare loan types (Conventional, FHA, VA, USDA, etc.).

☐ Choose between fixed-rate or adjustable-rate.

☐ Decide on a loan term (15, 20, or 30 years).

☑ 4. Lock in Your Interest Rate:

☐ Ask about rate-lock options.

☐ Understand how long your rate is locked.

☑ 5. Complete the Loan Application:

☐ Provide additional requested documents.

☐ Respond promptly to lender inquiries.

☐ Sign the loan estimate and disclosures.

☑ 6. Prepare for Closing:

☐ Review the closing disclosure (lists final costs and terms).

☐ Arrange for homeowners insurance.

☐ Complete the final walkthrough of the property.

☐ Bring your down payment and closing cost funds to closing.

Final Thoughts

Understanding your mortgage options, securing pre-approval, and locking in favorable interest rates are essential steps to buying your home with confidence. Your real estate agent and lender will guide you through the process, ensuring you make informed financial decisions.

In the next chapter, we'll explore how to find the perfect home, understand property types, and make competitive offers.

When You Have Will, You Have a Way. My Name Is Will. Let's make your home ownership dream a reality!

Chapter 6
Searching for Your New Home

The search for your dream home is both exciting and demanding. With the right approach and tools, you can find a home that meets your needs and fits your budget.

In this chapter, we'll cover:

- ✔ Defining your home criteria

- ✔ Utilizing online resources and listings

- ✔ Attending open houses and private showings

- ✔ Checklist: Home search essentials

Defining Your Home Criteria

Before you start viewing properties, it's essential to identify what you're looking for in a home. Clarifying your must-haves and nice-to-haves will save time and make your search more effective.

1. Location Preferences:
- Neighborhoods: Close to work, schools, or family?
- Commute: Proximity to major highways or public transportation.
- Amenities: Near parks, shopping centers, restaurants, or entertainment.
- School District: Important if you have or plan to have children.

2. Home Features:
- Type of Home: Single-family, townhouse, condo, or new construction.
- Size: Number of bedrooms and bathrooms.

• Floor Plan: Open concept, one-story, or multi-level.

• Lot Size: Small yard, large backyard, or acreage.

• Age of Home: New construction or an existing home with character.

3. Additional Preferences:

• Kitchen Style: Modern, gourmet, or open to the family room.

• Outdoor Spaces: Patio, pool, or garden.

• Garage: Number of spaces or preference for attached vs. detached.

• Energy Efficiency: Solar panels, smart home technology, or new appliances.

4. Future Needs:

• Resale Value: Is the area growing in value?

• Space for Growth: Extra room for a home office, gym, or guest room.

• Lifestyle Changes: Planning for children or elderly family members.

Utilizing Online Resources and Listings

Today's home search starts online, but knowing how to use digital tools effectively is key to narrowing your options before visiting in person.

1. Top Real Estate Platforms:

• HAR.com: The Houston Association of Realtors' platform with accurate, local listings.

• Zillow, Realtor.com, Redfin: National platforms with filters for price, location, and features.

• MLS Listings: Your real estate agent can provide exclusive access to the most up-to-date listings.

2. Setting Search Alerts:

Create automatic alerts with your criteria (price, location, number of bedrooms, etc.) to be notified immediately when new listings hit the market.

3. Virtual Tours and 3D Showings:

• Many listings now offer virtual tours and 3D walkthroughs, allowing you to explore homes from your couch.

• Use video tours for an initial screening before scheduling in-person showings.

4. Analyzing Listings:

• Photos: Look beyond staging—focus on layout and structure.

• Descriptions: Pay attention to keywords like "recently renovated," "new roof," or "motivated seller."

• Days on Market: Homes sitting for a long time may offer room for negotiation.

Attending Open Houses and Private Showings

Visiting homes in person is a critical step to see if a property truly fits your needs. Open houses and private showings allow you to experience the home's layout, condition, and surroundings.

1. Open Houses:

- A great way to explore homes without an appointment.

- Opportunity to meet listing agents and ask questions.

- Observe other buyers' reactions, which can indicate competition.

2. Private Showings:

- Personalized tours scheduled through your real estate agent.

- More time to inspect details and envision living in the space.

- Freedom to explore the home without distractions.

3. What to Observe During Visits:

- Neighborhood Vibe: Is it quiet, family-friendly, or busy?

- Natural Light: Check windows, orientation, and brightness.

- Storage Space: Look inside closets, attics, and garages.

- Condition of Major Systems: Roof, HVAC, plumbing, and appliances.

- Noise Levels: From neighbors, traffic, or nearby businesses.

4. Asking Important Questions:

- How old is the roof, HVAC system, and water heater?

- Are there any known issues with the property?

- What are the average utility costs?

- Are there HOA fees, and what do they cover?

Checklist: Home Search Essentials

Use this checklist to stay organized during your home search.

☑ 1. Define Your Criteria:

☐ Must-have features (bedrooms, bathrooms, yard size, etc.)

☐ Preferred neighborhoods and school districts

☐ Maximum budget (including taxes and HOA fees)

☑ 2. Set Up Search Tools:

☐ Create alerts on HAR, Zillow, or Realtor.com

☐ Follow listings on your agent's MLS portal

☐ Bookmark your top 5 choices for follow-up

☑ 3. Prepare for Showings:

☐ Schedule private tours with your agent

☐ Attend weekend open houses

☐ Take notes and rate each home (1–5 stars)

☑ 4. Evaluate Each Home Carefully:

☐ Exterior condition (roof, landscaping)

☐ Interior condition (floors, walls, appliances)

☐ Natural light and ventilation

☐ Noise levels inside and outside

☑ 5. Ask the Right Questions:

☐ Age of major systems (roof, HVAC)

☐ HOA rules and fees

☐ Recent upgrades or renovations

☐ Average utility costs

☑ 6. Review Neighborhood Details:

☐ Commute time to work or school

☐ Proximity to grocery stores and amenities

☐ Safety and crime rates

Final Thoughts

Searching for your new home should be a balance of excitement and careful consideration. By defining your needs, leveraging online resources, and attending showings with a discerning eye, you'll find the perfect place to call home.

When You Have Will, You Have a Way. My Name Is Will. Let's make your home search easy and successful!

Next up: Chapter 7 – Making an Offer and Negotiating Like a Pro.

Chapter 7
Making an Offer & Negotiating

You've found the perfect home—now it's time to secure it! Making an offer is a critical step where strategy and timing can make all the difference. Whether you're in a competitive market or negotiating on a home that's been sitting for a while, knowing how to craft a strong offer and negotiate effectively is essential.

In this chapter, we'll cover:

✅ Crafting a competitive offer

✅ Negotiation strategies

✅ Understanding contingencies

✅ Checklist: Steps after making an offer

Crafting a Competitive Offer

1. Understand Market Conditions:

Before making an offer, determine if you're in a buyer's or seller's market.

• Seller's Market: Homes sell quickly, often above asking price with multiple offers.

• Buyer's Market: Homes stay on the market longer, giving you more negotiation power.

• Balanced Market: Supply and demand are even, and offers typically align with market value.

2. Determine the Offer Price:

• Ask Your Agent for a Comparative Market Analysis (CMA): This report shows the selling prices of similar homes in the area, helping you make a data-driven offer.

• Evaluate the Home's Days on Market (DOM): A long DOM could signal room for negotiation, while a newly listed home may require a strong initial offer.

• Consider Recent Upgrades: Renovations, new appliances, or a new roof can add value.

3. Decide on Your Earnest Money Deposit (EMD):

• Typically 1–3% of the purchase price, EMD shows the seller you're serious.

• A higher deposit can make your offer more competitive, especially in a hot market.

4. Include a Strong Pre-Approval Letter:

• A pre-approval letter from your lender shows sellers that you're financially qualified to purchase their home, giving your offer more credibility.

5. Consider Offering Incentives:

• Flexible Closing Date: Aligning with the seller's timeline can be a deciding factor.

• Lease-Back Option: If the seller needs extra time to move, a lease-back can be attractive.

• Covering Closing Costs: Offering to pay part or all of the seller's closing costs can sweeten the deal.

Negotiation Strategies

Negotiation is where deals are won or lost. Understanding how to approach this step can help you secure the best price and terms.

1. Work with Your Agent:

Your agent is your advocate during negotiations, using their expertise to get you the best deal. Communicate your priorities clearly and trust their advice.

2. Start with a Strong Initial Offer:

In competitive markets, lowball offers can cause sellers to reject you outright. A strong, fair offer—backed by market data—signals that you are serious.

3. Be Willing to Walk Away:

Don't let emotions drive your decision. Know your maximum budget and stick to it. Sometimes, walking away is the best negotiation tactic.

4. Use Terms to Your Advantage:

Sometimes, terms can matter more than price. Offering a quicker closing, fewer contingencies, or more earnest money can make your offer stand out.

5. Respond Quickly to Counteroffers:

Negotiations can move fast, especially in a hot market. Responding promptly shows that you are serious and can prevent another buyer from stepping in.

6. Ask for Seller Concessions (When Appropriate):

If the inspection reveals issues or the home has been on the market for a while, consider asking the seller to cover closing costs, provide a home warranty, or make repairs.

Understanding Contingencies

Contingencies are conditions that must be met for the sale to close. They protect you from losing your earnest money if something goes wrong.

1. Common Contingencies:

• Financing Contingency: Protects you if your mortgage isn't approved.

• Inspection Contingency: Allows you to negotiate repairs or walk away if significant issues are found.

• Appraisal Contingency: Ensures the home's value matches the agreed price.

• Sale of Current Home Contingency: If you need to sell your existing home first.

2. Waiving Contingencies (Proceed with Caution):

In competitive markets, buyers sometimes waive contingencies to strengthen their offers. However, this comes with risks:

• Waiving the Inspection Contingency: You could be stuck with costly repairs.

• Waiving the Appraisal Contingency: You may have to pay out-of-pocket if the home doesn't appraise for the offer price.

Checklist: Steps After Making an Offer

☑ 1. Submit Your Offer:

☐ Work with your agent to draft a competitive offer.

☐ Include a pre-approval letter and earnest money deposit.

☐ Sign all necessary documents.

☑ 2. Review the Seller's Response:

☐ Accepted: Celebrate and prepare for the next steps!

☐ Counteroffer: Review and negotiate terms with your agent.

☐ Rejected: Decide if you want to submit a new offer or move on.

☑ 3. Handle the Earnest Money Deposit:

☐ Deliver your earnest money to the title company within the agreed time frame.

☑ 4. Schedule the Home Inspection:

☐ Book an inspector to assess the property's condition.

☐ Review the inspection report with your agent.

☐ Negotiate repairs or credits if necessary.

✓ 5. Finalize Your Mortgage:

☐ Submit the signed purchase agreement to your lender.

☐ Complete any additional lender requirements for final approval.

✓ 6. Order an Appraisal:

☐ Arrange for an appraisal through your lender.

☐ Review the results—if it's low, negotiate with the seller or reconsider the purchase.

✓ 7. Secure Homeowners Insurance:

☐ Obtain a policy before closing—your lender will require it.

✓ 8. Review the Closing Disclosure:

☐ Examine all costs and fees 3 days before closing.

☑ 9. Prepare for Closing:

☐ Conduct a final walk-through to ensure the home is in agreed condition.

☐ Bring necessary documents and identification to the closing.

☐ Sign all paperwork and receive the keys to your new home!

Final Thoughts

Making an offer is both an art and a science. A well-crafted, competitive offer with smart negotiation strategies can make all the difference in securing your dream home. By understanding contingencies and staying organized with your checklist, you'll be fully prepared for a successful transaction.

When You Have Will, You Have a Way. My Name Is Will. Let's negotiate your dream home together!

Next up: Chapter 8 — Closing the Deal: The Final Steps to Homeownership.

Chapter 8
The Home Inspection & Appraisal

The home inspection and appraisal are two of the most important steps in the home-buying process. These evaluations help ensure that your investment is sound, the property is in good condition, and the price aligns with its market value.

In this chapter, we'll cover:

- ✅ Importance of home inspections

- ✅ Selecting a qualified inspector

- ✅ Understanding the appraisal process

- ✅ Checklist: Inspection and appraisal

Importance of Home Inspections

A home inspection is a detailed examination of a property's condition, conducted by a licensed professional. It's your chance to identify potential issues before finalizing your purchase.

1. Why Home Inspections Matter:

• Uncover Hidden Problems: Inspectors can find issues not visible during a casual walkthrough (e.g., faulty wiring, plumbing leaks, or structural concerns).

• Negotiation Power: If problems are found, you can request repairs or credits from the seller.

• Safety Assurance: Detect hazards such as mold, carbon monoxide, or radon.

• Long-Term Savings: Catching issues early can prevent costly future repairs.

2. What Inspectors Check:

A standard home inspection covers:

• Structural Elements: Foundation, walls, and roof integrity

• Exterior: Siding, gutters, and windows

• Roofing: Condition of shingles and flashing

• Plumbing: Water pressure and potential leaks

• Electrical Systems: Outlets, wiring, and panels

• HVAC Systems: Heating and air conditioning functionality

• Interior: Floors, ceilings, and appliances

• Insulation and Ventilation: Energy efficiency and airflow

• Fireplaces and Chimneys: Proper ventilation and condition

Selecting a Qualified Inspector

1. How to Find a Reputable Home Inspector:

• Ask for Referrals: Your real estate agent, lender, or friends can recommend trustworthy inspectors.

• Check Credentials: Ensure the inspector is licensed and certified by a professional organization such as the American Society of Home Inspectors (ASHI) or the International Association of Certified Home Inspectors (InterNACHI).

• Review Experience: Inspectors with extensive experience, especially in the Houston area, are familiar with common local issues (e.g., foundation cracks due to soil conditions).

• Read Reviews: Check online reviews for customer feedback and professionalism.

2. Questions to Ask Your Home Inspector:

• How long have you been inspecting homes?

• Are you familiar with homes in the Houston area?

• What does your inspection include?

• Can I attend the inspection?

• How soon will I receive the inspection report?

3. Attend the Inspection:

Being present during the inspection helps you:

• Understand the Home's Condition: See potential issues firsthand.

• Learn Maintenance Tips: Inspectors often share valuable advice for maintaining your home.

• Ask Questions in Real-Time: Get clarification on any concerns immediately.

Understanding the Appraisal Process

A home appraisal is an evaluation of the property's market value conducted by a licensed appraiser. It protects both you and the lender by ensuring the home is worth the purchase price.

1. Why Appraisals Matter:

- Lender Requirement: Most lenders require an appraisal before approving your mortgage.

- Prevents Overpaying: Confirms that the price you're paying matches the home's market value.

- Impacts Loan Amount: If the appraisal is lower than the purchase price, your lender may reduce the loan amount.

2. How the Appraisal Process Works:

- Property Inspection: The appraiser visits the home to evaluate its condition, size, location, and features.

• Comparable Sales (Comps): The appraiser reviews recent sales of similar homes in the area.

• Market Trends: Local market conditions and trends are considered.

• Final Report: The appraiser provides a detailed report, including the home's market value.

3. What Happens If the Appraisal Is Low:

If the appraisal comes in lower than the agreed purchase price, you have options:

• Renegotiate the Price: Ask the seller to lower the price to meet the appraisal.

• Cover the Difference: Pay the difference out-of-pocket.

• Challenge the Appraisal: Request a review or a second appraisal if you believe there was an error.

• Walk Away: Use your appraisal contingency to exit the deal without penalty.

Checklist: Inspection and Appraisal

☑ Before the Inspection:

☐ Hire a licensed and experienced home inspector.

☐ Review the scope of the inspection.

☐ Attend the inspection to ask questions.

☑ During the Inspection:

☐ Take notes and photos of any issues.

☐ Ask about maintenance tips for the home.

☐ Clarify which issues are minor and which are serious.

☑ After the Inspection:

☐ Review the inspection report thoroughly.

☐ Request necessary repairs or credits from the seller.

☐ Decide whether to proceed, negotiate, or walk away.

✅ Before the Appraisal:

☐ Ensure the appraiser is licensed and familiar with the Houston market.

☐ Provide the appraiser with relevant property details (upgrades, renovations, etc.).

✅ During the Appraisal:

☐ Allow the appraiser to assess the home without interference.

☐ Highlight recent improvements that add value.

✅ After the Appraisal:

☐ Review the appraisal report carefully.

☐ If the value is lower than expected, explore renegotiation options.

☐ Confirm with your lender that the appraisal meets their requirements.

Final Thoughts

The home inspection and appraisal are essential steps that protect your investment and give you peace of mind. By selecting the right professionals and understanding the process, you can avoid costly surprises and make informed decisions.

When You Have Will, You Have a Way. My Name Is Will. I'll guide you every step of the way to ensure your home-buying experience is smooth and successful.

Next up: Chapter 9 – Closing the Deal: The Final Steps to Homeownership.

Chapter 9
Closing The Deal

Closing is the final and most exciting step in the home-buying process—it's when you officially become a homeowner. However, it's also a time when careful attention to detail is crucial to avoid last-minute surprises. In this chapter, we will walk you through:

- ✓ Finalizing mortgage details

- ✓ Reviewing closing disclosures

- ✓ The closing day process

- ✓ Checklist: Preparing for closing

Finalizing Mortgage Details

1. Locking in Your Interest Rate

Once your loan is approved, confirm with your lender that your interest rate is locked. A rate lock ensures that your interest rate won't increase before closing, which protects you from market fluctuations.

2. Reviewing Loan Terms

Make sure the loan terms (loan type, amount, and repayment period) match what was discussed during the pre-approval process. Confirm details such as:

- Loan type (fixed-rate, adjustable-rate, FHA, VA, or conventional)
- Monthly payment amount (including taxes and insurance)
- Interest rate and whether it's fixed or variable
- Loan term (e.g., 15, 20, or 30 years)

3. Providing Final Documentation

Lenders may request updated financial documents before closing to ensure nothing has changed. Be prepared to submit:

- Recent bank statements
- Proof of homeowner's insurance
- Final employment verification

4. Avoiding Major Financial Changes

Do not make large purchases, switch jobs, or open new credit lines before closing. Such changes can affect your credit score and loan approval.

Reviewing Closing Disclosures

1. What Is a Closing Disclosure (CD)?

A Closing Disclosure is a five-page form provided by your lender at least three business days before closing. It outlines the final terms of your loan, closing costs, and monthly payments.

2. How to Review Your Closing Disclosure:

Compare the CD with your original Loan Estimate (LE). Pay close attention to:

- Loan Terms: Loan amount, interest rate, and monthly payment.

- Projected Payments: Breakdown of principal, interest, property taxes, and homeowners insurance.

- Closing Costs: All fees, including lender fees, title insurance, and escrow deposits.

- Cash to Close: Total amount you need to bring to closing.

3. If There Are Errors:

- Contact your lender immediately if you spot discrepancies.

- Request corrections before closing day.

The Closing Day Process

1. What to Bring to Closing:

☑ A government-issued photo ID (e.g., driver's license or passport)

☑ Certified or cashier's check for your down payment and closing costs (if applicable)

☑ Proof of homeowners insurance

☑ Your Closing Disclosure (for reference)

☑ Any additional documents your lender requires

2. Who Will Be Present at Closing:

• Closing Agent or Escrow Officer: Facilitates the transaction.

• Title Company Representative: Ensures the property title is clear.

• Your Real Estate Agent: Supports and advises you.

• The Seller and Their Agent: If a traditional closing.

• Lender Representative: Sometimes present to address loan-related questions.

3. Documents You Will Sign:

• Promissory Note: Your agreement to repay the loan.

• Mortgage or Deed of Trust: Secures the loan with your home.

• Closing Disclosure: Confirms final loan terms and costs.

• Title Documents: Transfers property ownership to you.

• Affidavits and Declarations: Legal statements confirming property conditions and buyer information.

4. Funding and Keys:

• Once all documents are signed and the lender funds the loan, the title company records the deed with the county.

• You receive the keys to your new home!

Checklist: Preparing for Closing

☑ Before Closing:

☐ Review your Closing Disclosure carefully.

☐ Compare it to your Loan Estimate for discrepancies.

☐ Secure homeowners insurance and send proof to your lender.

☐ Arrange for a final walk-through of the property.

☐ Confirm the total amount for closing and how to pay (wire or cashier's check).

☐ Avoid new debts or major financial changes.

✅ **On Closing Day:**

☐ Bring a valid photo ID.

☐ Bring certified funds or proof of wire transfer.

☐ Bring all necessary documents (Closing Disclosure, insurance, etc.).

☐ Review all documents before signing.

☐ Keep copies of everything you sign.

✅ **After Closing:**

☐ Store your closing documents in a safe place.

☐ Set up automatic payments for your mortgage.

☐ Update your address with the post office, employers, and other services.

☐ Transfer utilities to your name.

☐ Celebrate—you are now a homeowner!

Final Thoughts

Closing on a home is a significant milestone, but it requires careful preparation and attention to detail. With the right guidance and a thorough review of your documents, you'll be ready to finalize your purchase smoothly.

When You Have Will, You Have a Way. My Name Is Will. I'll be with you from the first showing to the final signature, ensuring your path to homeownership is smooth and successful.

Next up: Chapter 10 – Settling Into Your New Home: Tips for a Smooth Transition.

Chapter 10
Moving Into Your New Home

Congratulations! You've closed on your new home and are ready for the next exciting step—moving in. Proper planning and organization will ensure a smooth transition. In this chapter, we will cover:

- ✅ Planning your move

- ✅ Setting up utilities and services

- ✅ Home maintenance tips

- ✅ Checklist: Post-move essentials

Planning Your Move

1. Create a Moving Timeline

- 6-8 Weeks Before Moving:

☐ Hire a moving company or reserve a rental truck.

☐ Notify your landlord (if renting) and schedule the end-of-lease walk-through.

☐ Begin sorting and decluttering your belongings.

• *4 Weeks Before Moving:*

☐ Pack non-essential items (e.g., seasonal clothes, books, and decorations).

☐ Collect important documents (e.g., mortgage papers, passports, medical records).

☐ Arrange for childcare or pet care for moving day.

• *2 Weeks Before Moving:*

☐ Label boxes by room for easy unpacking.

☐ Set up mail forwarding with USPS.

☐ Schedule disconnection and reconnection of utilities.

• *Moving Week:*

☐ Pack an essentials box (toiletries, medications, chargers, snacks, and important documents).

☐ Confirm arrangements with movers or rental services.

☐ Complete a final walk-through of your old home.

2. Hiring Movers vs. DIY Move:

• *Professional Movers:*

Ideal for long-distance moves or large households. Be sure to:

☑ Get multiple quotes.

☑ Read reviews and verify insurance coverage.

☑ Confirm the moving date and time.

• DIY Move:

Suitable for local moves and smaller loads. Be sure to:

☑ Rent an appropriately sized truck.

☑ Enlist friends or family to help.

☑ Gather packing supplies (boxes, tape, bubble wrap, and markers).

Setting Up Utilities and Services

1. Essential Utilities to Set Up:

☐ Electricity: Contact the local power company to ensure service begins on or before your move-in day.

☐ Water and Sewer: Arrange service through your city's public works department.

☐ Natural Gas: Contact the local provider for heating and cooking services.

☐ Trash and Recycling: Set up service through your city or a private provider.

2. Additional Services:

☐ Internet and Cable: Compare local providers for the best service and pricing. Schedule installation early to avoid delays.

☐ Home Security System: Consider installing a system for added safety.

☐ Lawn Care and Pest Control: Arrange services if not included in your HOA.

3. Updating Your Address:

☐ Post Office: Forward mail through USPS.

☐ Banks and Credit Cards: Update your billing address.

☐ Employer and Insurance Companies: Notify them of your new address.

☐ DMV: Update your driver's license and vehicle registration.

☐ Subscription Services: Change addresses for magazines, meal kits, and deliveries.

Home Maintenance Tips

1. Inspect Your Home:

• Check HVAC Filters: Replace if necessary.

• Test Smoke and Carbon Monoxide Detectors: Replace batteries.

• Inspect Windows and Doors: Ensure proper sealing to prevent drafts.

• Locate Emergency Shut-Offs: Know where to turn off gas, water, and electricity.

2. Set a Maintenance Schedule:

Monthly:

☐ Check HVAC filters.

☐ Inspect sinks and toilets for leaks.

☐ Test smoke alarms.

Seasonally:

☐ Clean gutters (spring and fall).

☐ Service HVAC systems before summer and winter.

☐ Winterize pipes before freezing weather.

Annually:

☐ Inspect the roof and foundation.

☐ Clean the chimney and fireplace.

☐ Pressure wash the driveway and siding.

3. Build a Home Maintenance Fund:

Set aside money for unexpected repairs. Experts recommend saving 1-3% of your home's value annually for maintenance.

Checklist: Post-Move Essentials

☑ First Week:

☐ Unpack essential rooms first (bedroom, kitchen, and bathroom).

☐ Inspect your property and document any issues.

☐ Secure your home (change locks, install security cameras if needed).

☐ Introduce yourself to neighbors.

✅ First Month:

☐ Review your HOA rules (if applicable).

☐ Organize important home documents.

☐ Test home systems (security alarms, appliances, and HVAC).

✅ Ongoing:

☐ Set up automatic payments for mortgage and utilities.

☐ Start a home improvement list for future projects.

☐ Join local community groups or neighborhood apps (e.g., Nextdoor).

Final Thoughts

Moving into your new home marks the beginning of an exciting chapter. By planning ahead, staying organized, and maintaining your property, you'll enjoy a smooth transition and protect your investment for years to come.

When You Have Will, You Have a Way. My Name Is Will. I'm here to help you beyond the closing table—whether it's settling in, maintaining your home, or planning your next move.

Chapter 11
Benefits of Hiring a Real Estate Agent for New Construction Homes

Purchasing a new construction home offers exciting possibilities—customization, modern features, and pristine living spaces. However, many buyers assume they don't need a real estate agent when purchasing directly from a builder. This is a common misconception! A real estate agent is your advocate, ensuring your best interests are protected throughout the entire process.

In this chapter, we will cover:

☑ Advocacy during builder negotiations

☑ Expertise in contract review

☑ Assistance with upgrades and customizations

☑ Knowledge of builder reputations

☑ Access to market comparisons

☑ Guidance through the construction timeline

☑ Ensuring proper inspections

☑ Navigating warranties and post-sale support

☑ Checklist: Selecting an agent for new construction

Advocacy During Builder Negotiations

1. Negotiating Beyond Price:

A skilled agent knows how to negotiate with builders for more than just the purchase price. They can secure valuable incentives such as:

- Closing cost assistance

- Free or discounted upgrades (e.g., appliances, flooring, or countertops)

- Extended warranties

- Lower interest rates through builder-lender promotions

2. Understanding Builder Contracts:

Builder contracts are designed to protect the builder—not the buyer. An agent can:

- Spot unfavorable clauses (e.g., construction delays or price escalation clauses)

- Negotiate more flexible terms

- Ensure your deposit is protected

Expertise in Contract Review

1. Builder Contracts vs. Standard Contracts:

Unlike resale properties, builder contracts often have terms that are complex and lengthy. Your agent can:

- Explain contingencies and timelines

- Ensure deadlines are fair and achievable

- Review cancellation policies and refund terms

2. Protecting Your Earnest Money:

Your agent will ensure the contract includes protection clauses that guarantee you get your earnest money back if the builder fails to meet their obligations.

Assistance with Upgrades and Customizations

1. Prioritizing Upgrades for Value:

Not all upgrades increase your home's future resale value. Your agent can help you:

- Focus on value-adding upgrades such as kitchens, bathrooms, and flooring.

- Negotiate for free or discounted upgrades.

2. Avoiding Overcapitalization:

Agents provide insight into what buyers in your area are looking for, helping you avoid spending too much on upgrades that won't yield a return on investment.

Knowledge of Builder Reputations

1. Builder Track Record:

A real estate agent with local experience will know which builders:

- Deliver on time
- Have a reputation for quality craftsmanship
- Are responsive to warranty issues
- Offer better after-sales service

2. Avoiding Problematic Builders:

Agents can alert you to builders who are known for cutting corners or delaying projects.

Access to Market Comparisons

1. Understanding Market Value:

Agents conduct comparative market analyses (CMAs) to help you:

- Avoid overpaying for your new home

- Understand how your chosen property compares to similar new and resale homes in the area

2. Evaluating Incentives:

Some builder incentives may seem attractive but aren't as beneficial as they appear. Your agent will compare these offers against industry standards to ensure you're getting a fair deal.

Guidance Through the Construction Timeline

1. Monitoring Construction Milestones:

New construction can take several months. Your agent will:

- Help you understand the construction process

- Keep the builder accountable for deadlines

- Schedule important walkthroughs (e.g., pre-drywall and final inspections)

2. Managing Delays:

If delays occur, your agent can:

- Communicate directly with the builder to resolve issues

- Negotiate adjustments to your contract timeline

- Ensure you are compensated if the builder fails to meet deadlines (if covered by the contract)

Ensuring Proper Inspections

1. Importance of Third-Party Inspections:

Even new construction homes can have defects. Your agent will recommend trusted third-party inspectors for:

- Pre-drywall inspections: Before walls are sealed, ensuring proper wiring, plumbing, and framing.

- Final inspections: Checking systems, appliances, and finishes before closing.

2. Addressing Inspection Issues:

If the inspector finds problems, your agent will:

- Negotiate repairs with the builder

- Ensure corrections are completed before closing

- Review the builder's warranty to confirm coverage for future issues

Navigating Warranties and Post-Sale Support

1. Understanding Builder Warranties:

Builders typically offer warranties covering different aspects of the home, such as:

- 1-Year Warranty: Covers workmanship and materials (e.g., drywall, paint, and trim).

- 2-Year Warranty: Covers systems like plumbing, electrical, and HVAC.

- 10-Year Warranty: Covers major structural issues.

2. Post-Sale Support:

Your agent will:

- Help you document issues for warranty claims.

- Advise you on how to address disputes with the builder.

• Provide recommendations for contractors for improvements or repairs.

Checklist: Selecting an Agent for New Construction

☑ Experience with New Construction: Look for an agent familiar with builder contracts and processes.

☑ Market Knowledge: Ensure they have insights into local builders and new home communities.

☑ Negotiation Skills: Ask about their experience securing incentives and upgrades.

☑ Inspection Guidance: Ensure they have a network of qualified third-party inspectors.

☑ Reputation and Reviews: Check online reviews and ask for references from previous new construction buyers.

☑ Availability: Confirm they can attend key milestones such as design meetings, walkthroughs, and closing.

Final Thoughts

Purchasing a new construction home is an exciting opportunity, but it comes with unique challenges. A knowledgeable real estate agent is your advocate from contract to closing, ensuring you get the best value, quality, and protection for your investment.

When You Have Will, You Have a Way. My Name Is Will. Let me guide you through your new construction journey with confidence and care.

Next: Chapter 12 – Avoiding Common Home-Buying Mistakes: What Every Buyer Should Know.

Chapter 12
Do's & Don'ts During the Home-Buying Process

The home-buying journey can be a complex and emotional process, filled with significant financial decisions and life changes. While it's exciting to envision your new home, navigating the steps thoughtfully is essential for a successful outcome. In this chapter, we will go over some crucial do's and don'ts to help guide you through the home-buying process with confidence.

DOs

1. Get Pre-Approved for a Mortgage

One of the first steps in the home-buying process is securing mortgage pre-approval. A pre-approval letter from a lender:

• Shows your seriousness as a buyer.

• Helps you understand your budget and avoid wasting time on properties outside your price range.

• Strengthens your offer when competing with other buyers.

By getting pre-approved, you ensure you're financially ready and can proceed confidently when the right home comes along.

2. Hire a Qualified Real Estate Agent

Hiring a professional real estate agent can significantly ease the process. An experienced agent will:

• Provide expert guidance throughout the home-buying process, from researching neighborhoods to negotiating offers.

• Advocate for your interests, ensuring you get the best deal.

• Handle the paperwork, helping you avoid legal pitfalls.

An agent will act as your trusted advisor, guiding you through decisions and helping you avoid costly mistakes.

3. Research Neighborhoods Thoroughly

Location is one of the most critical factors when buying a home. Researching potential neighborhoods will help you:

- Evaluate the convenience of proximity to work, schools, and amenities.

- Understand local property values to ensure you're investing in an area with potential for growth.

- Check crime rates and neighborhood reviews to ensure safety and comfort.

- Consider future developments that may impact your living experience.

Don't rush this process—spend time getting to know the neighborhood and its community.

4. Attend Multiple Open Houses

Open houses provide a valuable opportunity to:

• Get a feel for the property and its condition in person.

• Compare similar homes in the same price range and area.

• Ask questions about the property that may not be addressed in online listings.

Attending multiple open houses can also help you refine your wants and needs, giving you a clearer picture of what you're looking for in a home.

5. Read All Contracts Carefully

Before signing any documents, make sure to:

• Review every section of the contract. This includes purchase agreements, contingencies, and clauses related to repairs and inspections.

• Ask your agent to explain anything that you don't understand.

• Consult a lawyer if necessary for more complex legal language.

Taking the time to read all contracts carefully can save you from unpleasant surprises down the road.

6. Maintain Open Communication with Your Agent

Your real estate agent is there to help, so it's essential to:

• Be transparent about your wants, needs, and concerns to ensure they're working in your best interest.

• Keep them updated on any changes to your financial situation or home preferences.

• Ask questions if you're unclear about anything during the process. Your agent is your best resource.

Clear communication will ensure you stay on track and make informed decisions throughout the process.

7. Stay Within Your Budget

It's tempting to stretch your budget to secure your dream home, but it's essential to:

• Stick to your budget to avoid overextending financially.

• Consider long-term affordability. Ensure the mortgage payment and additional costs (insurance, taxes, utilities, etc.) are sustainable.

Staying within your budget ensures financial security, even after closing.

8. Plan for Additional Expenses

Beyond the down payment and mortgage, there are additional expenses that may arise, such as:

• Closing costs (e.g., title insurance, appraisal fees, inspection fees)

• Home improvements and repairs (even in new homes)

• Utility setup and other initial moving expenses.

Factor these additional costs into your budget to avoid surprises.

9. Be Patient and Flexible

The home-buying process can take time, and there may be unexpected delays or changes. Being patient:

• Helps you avoid rushing into a decision you might regret later.

• Allows you to explore different options, which could lead to a better home or better deal.

• Ensures you don't settle for less than what you want or need.

Stay open to flexibility, as what you initially envisioned may evolve as you explore more options.

10. Keep Your Financial Documents Organized

Throughout the home-buying process, you'll need various documents, including:

• Tax returns

• Bank statements

• Proof of income

• Credit history

Keeping these organized and easily accessible will speed up the process and reduce stress.

DON'Ts

1. Make Large Purchases Before Closing

Avoid making large purchases (e.g., new furniture, a car, or electronics) while your home purchase is in process. Large purchases can:

- Affect your credit score, possibly leading to mortgage approval issues.

- Increase your debt-to-income ratio, making you a riskier borrower in the eyes of your lender.

Wait until after closing to make big-ticket purchases.

2. Skip the Home Inspection

Even though new construction homes are typically in good condition, skipping a home inspection can:

- Overlook potential issues that may not be visible during a casual walkthrough.

- Leave you with costly repairs after closing.

A professional home inspector can identify hidden issues before you commit, saving you money and hassle.

3. Overlook Hidden Costs

In addition to the mortgage and down payment, there are other costs to consider:

- Homeowners' association (HOA) fees

- Property taxes

- Maintenance and upkeep

Don't forget to factor these into your financial planning to avoid stretching your budget.

4. Rush Into a Decision

It's easy to feel pressured when you find a home you like, but rushing into a decision can result in:

• Settling for less than what you truly want.

• Overpaying for the property without considering all factors.

• Purchasing a home with hidden issues that could have been discovered if you took more time to review it thoroughly.

Take the time to weigh all your options carefully before making an offer.

5. Neglect to Review the HOA Rules

If your home is part of a community with a homeowners' association (HOA), always review their rules and fees:

• HOA fees can add significantly to your monthly costs.

• HOA restrictions may limit certain home modifications or activities.

Understand these details before committing to the property.

6. Ignore Resale Value

While you may be buying your "forever home," it's essential to consider the resale value of your property. When buying a home, ask yourself:

• Will the property appreciate in value?

• Are there features that make it more attractive to future buyers?

Ignoring resale potential could impact your investment down the road.

7. Change Jobs During the Process

Job changes can cause lenders to question your financial stability. If possible, avoid:

• Changing jobs during the mortgage application process.

• Making career changes that could impact your income or employment history.

If a job change is unavoidable, discuss it with your lender before making any decisions.

8. Waive Contingencies Without Caution

Contingencies are clauses in your purchase contract that allow you to back out of the deal under certain conditions, such as:

• Failing the home inspection.

• The appraisal coming in too low.

While waiving contingencies might make your offer more appealing, it exposes you to unnecessary risks. Carefully weigh the pros and cons before deciding to waive contingencies.

9. Forget to Budget for Closing Costs

In addition to the down payment, closing costs typically range from 2% to 5% of the home's purchase price. These include:

- Title insurance
- Appraisal fees
- Attorney fees

Make sure you have enough funds available to cover these costs at closing.

10. Disregard Future Life Plans

Consider how your home purchase fits into your long-term plans:

- Will the home accommodate future family needs or life changes?

- Is it in a location that fits with your career, social, and lifestyle goals?

Purchasing a home is a long-term investment, so take the time to think about how it fits into your overall future plans.

Conclusion

Purchasing a home is an exciting, often life-changing decision, but it requires careful thought and preparation. By following the do's and avoiding the don'ts in this chapter, you will be well on your way to making informed and successful choices. Take your time to gather information, communicate openly with your agent, and carefully assess each decision along the way.

Encouragement for Prospective Homeowners

Remember, homeownership is a journey. Be patient with the process, and don't be afraid to ask questions or seek help along the way. Each step you take will bring you closer to finding a place you'll be proud to call home.

Final Thoughts and Resources

This guide has covered the essential aspects of the home-buying process. To assist you further, you can consult with your real estate agent, mortgage broker, or financial planner to ensure you're making the best decisions based on your unique situation.

When You Have Will, You Have a Way. My Name Is Will. I'm here to help guide you through the home-buying process with confidence and ease.

THE ART & ARTISTS

HOME OWNERSHIP IS CLOSER THAN YOU THINK: WHEN YOU HAVE WILL, YOU HAVE A WAY by Willie Adolph of Texas is your set of keys to the front doors of the lap of luxury. Whether you're dreaming of your first home or finally ready to stop renting and start building equity, this empowering  guide by Houston's real estate guru Willie Adolph will help you unlock the future you deserve.

Published with the assistance of BePublished.org, this July 2025 release is more than a how-to book. It is a *roadmap* to homeownership in the place that is just right for you. No more settling! No more giving up! This luxury homes specialist has years of experience putting hundreds of people in homes by listing and selling properties in record-breaking time, achieving the highest home sale rates for clients. Willie, a certified Real Estate Negotiator (RENE), Mortgage Loan Officer (MLO), licensed Financial Advisor, and two-time Eagle Award winner for helping fellow realtors and his community, walks you step-by-step through assessing your readiness, demystifying the financial details, and making confident, informed decisions every step of the way.

Learn how to understand your financial health; prepare for mortgage approval; avoid common pitfalls; and navigate today's real estate market with ease.

Whether in **ebook, softcover, or hardback**, **HOME OWNERSHIP IS CLOSER THAN YOU THINK: WHEN YOU HAVE WILL, YOU HAVE A WAY** by Willie Adolph is available worldwide — so you can start your journey anywhere, anytime.

Get your copy today from your favorite online or bricks-and-mortar bookseller — and take that first step toward turning the key and opening your very own front door. Because, when you have Mr. Will, you *always* have a way to live the American dream.

Willie & Tikila Adolph are a powerhouse Kingdom couple who have been married for over 25 years and have worked together in business for over 20+ years. Their journey is a testament to love, faith, and teamwork, inspiring couples to thrive in both marriage and entrepreneurship.

Together, Willie and Tikila have achieved incredible success across various industries:

• Real Estate Professionals: As the founders of The Adolph Group, they specialize in luxury and commercial listings, sales, and helping families find their dream homes. They are known for their transparency, integrity, and unmatched dedication to their clients.

• Educators and Mentors: With a combined passion for teaching, they lead legal and contract classes, guide real estate students, and coach couples on business growth. Their mission is to empower others to pursue their dreams with confidence.

• Travel Entrepreneurs: Through WTA Travel Agency, they help clients worldwide create unforgettable travel experiences. As certified members of CLIA, they hold Dream Maker, Vacation Builder, Group and Luxury Cruise certifications.

- Community Leaders: Willie and Tikila are deeply committed to their community, often mentoring couples, young professionals, and families. They believe in giving back and building a legacy of faith and generosity.

Beyond their professional accomplishments, Willie and Tikila are proud parents of four children, grandparents to two, and doting caregivers to their furbaby, Dash. Their partnership is built on faith, love, and a shared vision of success.

Quote from the Authors:

"Marriage is a journey of compromise, faith, and unconditional love. Together, you can overcome anything and build a beautiful life. It's okay to have it all."

With over two decades of experience in real estate, business, and ministry, Willie T. Adolph, Jr. and Tikila Antoinette Adolph have built a legacy rooted in service, education, and empowerment. Their journey, which began in 2001 as mortgage loan officers, quickly evolved  into a shared mission of helping individuals and families achieve financial stability and homeownership.

As licensed real estate professionals, mentors, national authors, ordained ministers, travel advisors, and philanthropists,  Willie and Tikila are not just industry leaders—they are passionate educators and advocates who have dedicated their lives to equipping others with the knowledge and confidence to succeed in real estate and beyond. Their expertise spans across home buying and selling, investment strategies, credit restoration, insurance, and business development, making them sought-after speakers, mentors, and advisors.

Together, they have built a thriving real estate team and set a bold vision: to serve over 100 families annually through real estate transactions, not simply for profit, but with a genuine desire to make a lasting impact on the lives of their clients. Transparency, honesty, and integrity are the foundation of their business, ensuring that every interaction reflects their deep-seated belief in ethical leadership and trust.

Beyond real estate, the Adolphs are devoted parents, grandparents, and community leaders. Their faith is the cornerstone

of their personal and professional lives, guiding their marriage, business, and philanthropic efforts. They regularly give back through free real estate seminars, youth sports initiatives, and mentorship programs, fostering opportunities for others to achieve their dreams.

Through their self-employed business, which they have operated together since 2001, Willie and Tikila have cultivated a reputation as leaders who serve with purpose, passion, and compassion. Their unwavering dedication to faith, family, and financial empowerment continues to inspire those they encounter, making them a true powerhouse couple in the world of real estate and beyond.

💼 Areas of Expertise:

✔ Real Estate Sales & Training | ✔ Homeownership & Investment Strategies | ✔ Business Growth & Mentorship ✔ National Speaking Engagements | ✔ Faith-Based Leadership & Ministry | ✔ Travel Planning & Lifestyle Services | ✔ Group travel & cruise experts

👪 Family First: Proud parents of four children, loving grandparents, and pet parents to their beloved furbaby, Dash Adolph.

🌍 Mission Statement: To educate, empower, and uplift individuals and families through faith, integrity, and financial freedom.

For more about Willie and Tikila, or to connect with them to begin the next phase of your Real Estate journey, call (281) 451-7087 or visit bit.ly/theadolphs and TheAdolphs.com.